MONEY
Burden or Blessing?

Donald A. Leggett

CLEMENTS PUBLISHING
Toronto

Clements Publishing
6021 Yonge St, Box 213
Toronto, Ontario
M2M 3W2 Canada
www.clementspublishing.com

ISBN-10: 1-894667-86-7
ISBN-13: 978-1894667-86-9

Contents

I.   Introduction

In his book *Money, Sex and Power*, R. Foster maintains that these three issues are "inseparably intertwined". Money manifests itself as power, sex is used to acquire both money and power, and power is often called the "best aphrodisiac". All three are discussed extensively in the Old Testament and are part of the lived-out reality of faith, though sadly in our current culture, professing Christians sometimes falter in these areas. When this happens, God's name is blasphemed (Num. 15:30). It is more important than ever for today's people of faith to live faithfully.

Our intention is to look at some passages in the O.T. and see how the teachings there correspond with the N.T. or add vital biblical revelation to it for our consideration. There is both a dark side and a bright side to wealth in both testaments. A few preliminary remarks will demonstrate these two strata of texts.

The Dark Side of Wealth

The scriptures never underestimate the peculiar temptations connected with wealth. Wealth often competes with God for our attention and energy (Jer. 9:23). It promises security and happiness that can only be fulfilled by the Lord. It has a deceptive power that seduces (Mark 4:19). It competes with God for the love (I Tim. 6:10), honor (Jer. 9:23), and trust (I Tim. 6:17) of his people. Money tempts towards pride, false security and apostacy (Prov. 28:11; 18:11; 30:9a). When confronted with the clear choice between God and wealth, many choose wealth (Matt. 6:24; Mark 10:23; Luke 12:21).

The Bright Side of Wealth

There is a lighter and brighter side to wealth. Material blessings are to be a ladder by which our thoughts are raised to God in gratitude for the furnished table that he has provided (Ps. 23:5). They are part of the 'everything' the Lord has given us for our enjoyment (I Tim. 6:17). However, they also come with responsibilities attached, in that the law specifies ways in which generosity towards, and care for the poor are to be shown. In this manner God's people participate in his work through their material gifts (Lev. 19:9ff; Deut. 15:9ff).

II.   Wealth in the Old Testament

Deuteronomy 8: 1-18

Verse 10 tells us that material abundance is intended to be a source of praise and thankfulness. But it is also a source of temptation to "forget the LORD your God". It needs to be said that 'forget' is a verb which is best understood as a *moral* act rather than a *mental* one. The dark side of wealth consists of its ability to lead to significant lifestyle changes, as in vss.12-14:

> "Otherwise, when you eat and are satisfied, when you build fine houses and settle down, and when your herds and flocks grow large and your silver and gold increase and all you have is multiplied, then your heart will become proud and you will forget the LORD your God."

The various forms of wealth mentioned in this passage taken together may lead the heart to pride which produces a spirit of independence from God. Prov. 30:7-9 echoes these thoughts from Deut. and adds the possibility that material well-being may lead to a spirit of self-sufficiency. Strikingly it is in the form of a prayer:

> "Two things I ask of you, O LORD; do not refuse me before I die: Keep falsehood and lies far from

me; give me neither poverty nor riches, but give only my daily bread. Otherwise, I may have too much and *disown* you and say, 'Who is the LORD?' or I may become poor and steal, and so *dishonor* the name of my God."

Extending the theme of the heart becoming proud, Deut. 8:17 warns us, "You may say to yourself, 'My power and the strength of my hands have produced this wealth for me.'" If we think thus in our hearts, we are sadly and tragically mistaken! "But remember the LORD your God, for it is he who gives you the ability to produce wealth" (vs. 18).

In summary, this passage argues for the following three principles: (1) If, in the providence of God we are given much, so that we eat and are satisfied, we should give praise to God, no one needs to have a guilty conscience for acquiring wealth; (2) Remember that there is a potential in wealth to ruin as well as to bless and to turn our hearts away from God; (3) In the final analysis, God gives us the ability to acquire wealth. Yes, we may have worked hard and thereby become wealthy, but if our circumstances or physical or mental abilities had been different, then we may not have become so successful.

Deuteronomy 26:1-11

Wright remarks, that the whole chapter is "a wonderful presentation of covenant *grace,* covenant *obedience,* and covenant *blessing*." Deuteronomy, *New International Biblical Commentary*, p. 270. For our purpose, we will call attention to the ceremonial law described in this passage by noting the emphasis on the gift of land and the firstfruits of the land as coming from the gracious hand of the covenant God. The people have entered the Promised Land (26:1) and this is seen to be the result of the divine promise and

8

the divine gift. The acknowledgement is made in vss 5-10 that the blessings of nature (firstfruits) are the result of God's redemptive activity in the Exodus (26:8-10). In a remarkable way the passage connects the facts of *history* from the past to the present and a *theology* of redemption with a *personal experience* of God's blessing. It brings together a blend of corporate blessing (vs. 9 - *us*) with individual blessing (vs. 10 – "that you have brought *me*").

Proverbs 3:9-10

This is one of the best-known texts in the O.T. pertaining to our subject. It is preceded by statements which stress trusting God and not leaning on 'your own understanding' (vs. 5). "Do not be wise in your own eyes; fear the Lord and shun evil" (vs. 7). Do we consider that it may be a serious evil when we fail to honor God with our substance? There is a connection with what follows:

> "Honor the Lord with your wealth, with the first-fruits of all your crops; then your barns will be filled to overflowing, and your vats will brim over with new wine."

The first and most obvious principle taught here is that giving to God is a way of honoring him. The highest calling of a believer is to bring honor and glory to God. If earthly treasures hold sway over our hearts we will not take this seriously and financial giving to the kingdom of God will not be a very high priority. Treasure on earth will be seen to be vastly more desirable than treasure in heaven (Matt. 6:19-20).

The reason God regulates the use of money is so that we will use it properly and demonstrate that God is more precious to us than what money can buy. A godly use of money means we are making much of God. It is a means of making visible the location of the heart. We are *entrusted* with wealth. "Wealth and honor come from you" (I Chron. 29:12a).

In Prov. 3:9 God is to be honored with our firstfruits. Firstfruits were the acknowledgement of redemption from Egypt (Deut. 26:1-10). Bringing the firstfruits was an act of faith since there was no automatic guarantee of God's continuing supply of material blessings thereafter. The heart desirous of honoring God has this promise. "Those who honor me I will honor, but those who despise me will be despised" (1 Sam. 2:30b; cf. Heb. 6:10). By honoring God through our giving we show our faith in his providence and promise, our love towards God, our gratitude for his goodness, and our preference of serving him instead of money (Matt. 6:24).

If we do not honor God by our giving, then we dishonor him by showing that we love the world more than God and we give lie to the song, "I'd rather have Jesus, than silver or gold; I'd rather have Jesus than riches untold". We need to experience what Prov. 11:24 teaches us: "One man gives freely, yet gains even more; another withholds unduly, but comes to poverty."

I Chronicles 29:10-18

This is one of the key statements in the O.T. acknowledging God as both source and owner of all our wealth. In vss. 10-13 we read David's song of praise to the Lord, who is "the greatness and the power and the glory and the majesty and the splendor; for everything in heaven and earth is yours... Wealth and honor come from you...Now, our God, we give you thanks, and praise your glorious name."

Earlier portions of chapter 29 describe the gifts given by king David and the leaders of families and officers and commanders used in constructing the temple. David's praise prayer continues from vs. 14. David is humbled ("Who am I") as are his people to be able to give as generously as they did. He describes himself and his people and their forefathers as 'aliens and strangers'. They are an insignificant people "whose days on earth are like a shadow" (vs. 15). This humility moved David to declare that the abundance which they gave for building Yahweh a temple "comes from your hand and all of it belongs to you" (vs. 16). God *tests the heart* by his people's giving and David affirms before God that he and his people have not only given generously but *willingly* (vs. 17). David then prays that the desire to give which comes from their heart may continue forever and as such "keep their hearts loyal to you" (vs. 18).

Giving generously and willingly requires grace. Acknowledging God as the giver of every good and perfect gift and the absolute owner of all we have is not a piece of bookshelf theology. It is as definitive a test of our love and devotion to God as anything can be.

Psalm 49

As a wisdom psalm the intended audience is universal: "Hear this, all you peoples; listen, all who live in this world, both low and high, rich and poor alike:" (vss. 1-2). The wicked "trust in their wealth and boast of their great riches" (vss. 5-6). But death is the great equalizer of rich and poor. The wealthy who trust in themselves will also die and leave behind their "princely mansions" which characterized their earthly lives (vss. 13-14). But the psalmist and all those he represents declare that, "God will redeem my life (soul) from the grave; he will surely *take me to himself*" (vs. 15). The psalmist urges all of us "not to be overawed (and fearful) when a man grows rich, and when the splendor of his house increases" (vs. 16) since the wealthy have no advantage when it comes to dying. The psalm seeks to counteract the powerful influence of the wealthy (vs. 5). The issue in this psalm is not wealth itself, but rather those who use it as an alternative to God, i.e. trust in themselves (vs. 13). No one will find his or her ultimate security in wealth.

The scriptures do not attack or downgrade wealth as unimportant or evil. In particular, books like Proverbs assume the goodness of God's gifts in creation. Only in this light can wealth be seen as a consequence of and congruent to wisdom and righteousness. Equally, poverty is congruent with and a consequence of folly and wickedness. The basic thrust of the psalm is found in the concluding statement "A man who has riches without understanding is like the beasts that perish" (vs. 20).

Malachi 3:8-12

According to G.B. Shaw, money is indeed the most important thing in the world. "When money speaks, truth is silent". Sadly this is often the case. But is this not one area in which the people of God are to be significantly different? Is it not true that when a person is converted, so also is his or her pocketbook? It should be true because giving is an evidence of love and we love him "because he first loved us" (I John 4:19). Giving therefore makes us like God. The scriptures teach that giving is a form of honoring the Lord. Giving is also an activity whereby we share in the work of God and his kingdom becomes our work (Ps. 90:16-17).

God is the source of all we have (Hag. 2:8). When we deny this truth in our daily lives, we engage in a practical form of idolatry. Sometimes within the covenant nation this idolatry took the form of looking to Canaanite fertility deities as the source of material well-being (Hos. 2:8). At other points it was a more humanistic type of idolatry. "My power and the strength of my hands have produced this wealth for me" (Deut. 8:17). In either case, it was a slap in the face of the living God.

It is instructive that Malachi's teaching about money (tithes and offerings) is given as an illustration of the need to repent. So often repentance is viewed as an emotional thing, feeling a certain degree of sorrow over sin. Here it is clearly volitional. It is a change of *attitude*, manifesting itself in a change of *action*. Faith always influences both our affections and our actions. One such action is to acknowledge by the practical means of the tithe and offering that everything belongs to the Lord. Setting aside a portion symbolizes that *all* is given by God.

Sin, the Great Robbery

To sin is to engage in the great robbery (vs. 8). Although the cattle upon a thousand hills belong to God and he is not in need of our gifts (Ps. 50:10), failure to bring the tithes and offerings is not just robbing God of that which rightfully belongs to him, but such sin and disobedience rob the Lord of the honor and the glory which he as sovereign is due (Ps. 96:8; Prov. 3:9). Giving honors the Lord through obedience, recognition, and acknowledgement of him as the source of all that we have. God cares about the heart, not the money. Failure to give the tithes and offerings, part of which went to the Levites to support them in the work which they did in serving at the tent of meeting, shows how little heart the people had for the worship of God.

Since the tithes were at least partly used for the poor (Deut. 14:28-29; 26:12), it can be said as well that the poor are robbed, and since God so closely identifies with the poor, he is thereby defrauded. Tithing is God's way of involving his people in his own redemptive activity in his concern for the poor. Just as he shares his blessings with his people, so those who benefit from those blessings must share them with those who are less fortunate.

Encouragement to Repent

The prophet connects his command to repent with a gracious promise: "Return to me and I will return to you" (Mal. 3:7; cf. Zech. 1:3). The latter idea stresses the intention behind the action. Even though a persistent pattern of turning from the Lord and his ordinances has characterized Israel in the past, it is not too late if they will turn to him in repentance:

> "God is said to *return* to us, when he ceases to demand the punishment of our sins, and when he lays aside the character of a judge, and makes himself known to us as a Father." Calvin, *Twelve Minor Prophets*, vol. 5, p. 582).

It is an encouragement for the wayward wanderer to return home. "Come near to God and he will come near to you" (James. 4:8). It is only sin that separates from God and causes him to hide his face (Isa. 59:2). No one, however, can and will repent apart from an awareness of sin and an encouragement that upon repentance they will be graciously received (Isa. 55:7).

The bad news (sin) always precedes the good news (the gospel). Thus the tragic blindness of the people's hasty replies to the prophet's exhortations, "What have we done that we need to repent?" (Mal. 2:14, 17; 3:6, 8, 13). This implies that they feel no need to turn to God. They are pure in their own eyes (Prov. 30:12). The Jews at the time of Christ had the same attitude when they were urged to repentance by John the Baptist. They were warned not to think that they did not need to repent because they had Abraham as their father (Matt. 3:9).

II. WEALTH IN THE OLD TESTAMENT

Many are ready to acknowledge themselves in a va, and general way to be sinners, but fewer ever get down repent of *specific* sins. To enable the rich young ruler to see his true need of a Savior, Jesus warned him specifically against the sin of covetousness (Luke 18:18-27). The prophet Malachi likewise lays *specific* charges of sin against the people in the area of tithes and offerings.

In preaching repentance, he addresses the entire nation (3:9a) since all the people were apparently guilty of giving God their second best, He tells them to bring the *whole* tithe into the storehouse (3:10a). The word "whole" is being emphasized because *part* of the requirements of the law of tithes was being followed but not the whole:

> "We then see that it is no new or unusual thing for men to pretend to do the duties they owe to God, and at the same time to take away from him what is his own, and to transfer it to themselves, and that manifestly, so that their impiety is evident, though it be covered by the veil of dissimulation." Calvin, *Twelve Minor Prophets*, vol. 5, p. 589.

If we wish to experience the blessing of God, we will need to be concerned with specific details in the perform-ance of our duties.

By failing to honor the Lord in bringing their tithes and offerings, the Levites who served the Lord were without their proper portions and withdrew from the service of the temple (Neh. 13:10). Undoubtedly this is what is meant by the phrase, "that there may be food in my house" (Mal. 3:10). The principle that "those who preach the gospel should receive their living from the gospel" is being vio-lated (I Cor. 9:14).

Although the priests had shown themselves to be un-trustworthy in God's service (Mal. 2:8), the Lord would not allow his people to disobey the law requiring their support.

Their full tithes and gifts had to be brought to the store-house; i.e., a room within the temple for the storage of such gifts (II Chron. 31:11; Neh. 10:38-39).

God invited the people of that day to test him! This is a reversal of common biblical usage. It is normally God who tests man in the O.T. (Ps. 26:2; Prov. 17:3). There are only a few instances of men being invited to test God; i.e. to prove his claims and justify his commands (Isa. 7:11-12; Judg. 6:36-40). Of course it is true that the proof of the pudding is in the eating. The psalmist who recounts his own experience of the goodness of the Lord invites his hearers to taste and see that the Lord is good (Ps. 34:8). There are warnings, however, against a wrong kind of testing of God (cf. Ps. 95:8-11).

A note of caution and reserve is required here. Certainly the text contains no ironclad formula for material success. It is not an open-ended promise to bless materially:

> "It cannot be reduced, as sometimes happens, to a formula for success in business: if you give such and such, you can be sure that your profits will rise phenomenally year after year! The principle is rooted more in the health of the relationship a person has with God." P. Craigie, *Twelve Prophets*, vol. 2, p. 244.

Although the text from Malachi about tithing must be rejected as a formula for material prosperity, there are important principles arising from it. True faith and giving are intertwined. Little faith and little giving logically go together (Matt. 6:30). To be sparing in our faith and giving will result in our receiving sparingly. Therefore Paul writes "whoever sows sparingly will also reap sparingly; and whoever sows generously will also reap generously" (II Cor. 9:6).

II. WEALTH IN THE OLD TESTAMENT

Proverbs

Money in both testaments is often an alternative god, just as Jesus said (Matt. 6:24). Proverbs "analyzes the topic of wealth in terms of its dangers, limitations, value and management". B. Waltke, *Proverbs*, vol. 1, NICOT, p. 103.

The danger of money is its ability to replace God in the human heart. It is a rival in that it may become an alternative source of security and trust. Rather than complete dependence on the Lord, "the wealth of the rich is their fortified city" (10:15a). The danger for the rich man is that he "may be wise in his own eyes" (28:11a).

The limitations of wealth are graphically spoken of in Prov. 11:4: "Wealth is worthless in the day of wrath, but righteousness delivers from death." This text is found in a passage which extols the value of righteousness and the impotence and worthlessness of riches (11:3-8). Security comes through righteousness alone and puts the lie to the wicked person's vain pursuit of wealth. The parallel between 11:4 and 10:2 is interesting. The former declares wealth to be worthless while the latter declares ill-gotten treasures to be of no value. Both texts end with the phrase: "righteousness delivers from death."

In summarizing what Foster calls the dark side of wealth, the following statements and passages need to be addressed:

1. Wealth may blind a person and cause them to *forget* God (Deut. 8: 10-14).
2. Wealth may tempt one to *disown* God (Prov. 30:8-9).
3. Failure to give the O.T. tithe was described as *robbing* God and in such case repentance was absolutely necessary (Mal. 3:6-12).
4. Many passages speak of the *idolatry* of wealth (Ps. 49:6; Deut. 31:20; Jer. 9:23-24; Prov. 18:11).

5. Jealousy over the wealth and well-being of the wicked within Israel (Ps. 73:1-14) was a leading source of *envy* and *discontent*. It may become a source of stress and anxiety for the wealthy person as well: "Whoever loves money never has money enough; whoever loves wealth is never satisfied with his income. This too is meaningless" (Eccles. 5:10).

6. Wealth is bankrupt to provide what it claims it can do because it is basically *unstable*. "Do not wear yourself out to get rich; have the wisdom to show restraint. Cast but a glance at riches, and they are gone, for they will surely sprout wings and fly off to the sky like an eagle" (Prov. 23:4-5). In the N.T. Paul speaks of "wealth which is uncertain" (I Tim. 6:17).

7. Several texts in Proverbs address the issue of having an *excessive eagerness* to obtain wealth. "A faithful man will be richly blessed, but one eager to get rich will not go unpunished" (Prov. 28:20); "Death and destruction are never satisfied, and neither are the eyes of man" (Prov. 27:20). An excessive desire to get rich may lead a person to engage in fraud in buying and selling. The picture of merchants using dishonest scales is mentioned several times (Prov. 11:1; 20:10). "The Lord detests differing weights and dishonest scales do not please him" (Prov. 20:23; Amos 8:4-6; Mic. 2:1-2). Eagerness which exceeds all bounds leads to oppression often in the legal system: "Do not move an ancient boundary stone or encroach on the fields of the fatherless, for their Defender (Redeemer God) is strong; he will take up their case against you" (Prov. 23:10-11). Moreover, "A fortune made by a lying tongue is a fleeting vapor and a deadly snare" (Prov. 21:6).

The words of the prophet Jeremiah are a serious indictment against defrauding workers of their wages (Jer.

22:13-17). This practice continued in the later period of O.T. history:

> "So I will come near to you for judgment. I will be quick to testify against sorcerers, adulterers and perjurers, against those who defraud laborers of their wages, who oppress the widows and the fatherless, and deprive aliens of justice, but do not fear me" (Mal. 3:5).

Acts of fraud and social injustice point to a fundamental breakdown in the covenant relationship. If those who defraud do not fear God (Ps. 130:4) this may indicate there is no genuine relationship resulting from the wonder of forgiveness. Finally, there is the danger inherent in wealth of despising the poor and being caught up in pride. Economic life in the O.T. is to be seen as a way of serving God and neighbor. Why else would there be so many statements in Israel's law codes which touch on economic life? When the poor are oppressed God is denied (Prov. 14:31).

An extension of oppressing the poor is mocking the poor (Prov. 17:5a). The verb 'oppresses' is sometimes rendered 'slanders' or 'scoffs at' as in Ps. 2:4 where the NIV translates it "scoffs". This behavior means to deny the significance, worth, or ability of someone or something:

> "...the creation of humankind functions as the philosophical basis for social ethics" (Waltke, *Proverbs*, vol. 1, p. 607).

The poor are treated with contempt and derision rather than viewed as image bearers of God. Proverbs 17:5b speaks of the rich, who "gloat over the disasters" of the poor and in doing so they "will not go unpunished." It seems clear that the rich are calloused, unsympathetic and hostile toward the poor person's economic adversity. All this type of behavior is really an attack on and insult to their Creator. There are many passages in Proverbs which warn against unkind and merciless responses to the plight of the poor.

Sometimes the oppression of the poor by the rich is "to increase their wealth" (22:16). Such exploitation is sometimes accomplished through the courts. Retribution in that case will return on the heads of the rich. "Do not exploit the poor because they are poor and do not crush the needy in court, for the Lord will take up their case and will plunder those who plunder them" (22:22-23). The rich are exhorted to be generous in which case they will be blessed, because they "share (their) food with the poor" (22:9).

One of the ways to legitimately increase one's economic well-being is to work hard and to avoid laziness. These two things are often contrasted, as in Prov. 10:4-5: "Lazy hands make a man poor, but diligent hands bring wealth. He who gathers crops in summer is a wise son, but he who sleeps during harvest is a disgraceful son" (cf. Prov. 6:6-8, which addresses the sluggard). Sluggards are often contrasted with the diligent. "The sluggard craves (desires) and gets nothing, but the desires of the diligent are fully satisfied" (13:4).

'Better Than' Sayings

Proverbs mentions several things which are better than wealth:

Wisdom

"How much better to get wisdom than gold, to choose understanding rather than silver" (16:16). Waltke comments:

"Wisdom has inestimable superiority to precious
metals because it bestows spiritual virtues along
with material benefits (see 3:13-18). Wealth without
wisdom is vulgar and greedy and/or may be due to
ruthless individualism" (*Proverbs*, vol. 2, p. 25).

Wisdom bestows a full array of positive spiritual virtues
such as we have been discussing. Godly wisdom:

"will save you from the ways (life styles) of wicked
men" (2:12) and "it will save you also from the
adulteress, from the wayward wife with her seduc-
tive words, who has left the partner of her youth and
ignored the covenant she made before God"
(2:16,17).

A Good Name

"A good name is more desirable than great riches; to be
esteemed is better than silver or gold" (22:1). In this proverb, as with the first, though there is a godly use of wealth
it is being downplayed in favor of a good name:

"The latter (good name) is the outward expression
of the person's inner wisdom. In this positive comparison, material wealth is esteemed as good, but
the social quality of a good reputation and its causes
is better. Wealth can be attained without virtue
(11:16, 28), but not a good name. Wisdom gives
both (3:13-14). Moreover, wealth can pass away
unexpectedly and quickly (23:5), but a good name
endures (10:7). Waltke, *Proverbs*, vol. 2, p. 199.

The Fear of the LORD

"Better a little with the fear of the LORD than great wealth with turmoil" (15:16). Here we see that outward circumstances (a little) do not negate the great religious truth of Prov. 1:7. The fear of the Lord is to be preferred, even in a situation of adverse outward circumstance over the inner turmoil which sometimes accompanies wealth with its stresses. God is not to be treasured because of what he gives us. This proverb assumes the wicked have material well being and the righteous do not. Poverty with spiritual reality (the fear of the Lord) is better than great wealth with turmoil (15:16). Turmoil is understood as the frenzied, stormy, panicky activity which often accompanies the wealthy in their agitation over and eagerness for riches. The Hebrew term translated turmoil, in the this passage may be inward, as it is in Amos 3:9, where it is found in combination with the word "oppression": "Assemble yourselves on the mountains of Samaria; see the great *unrest* within her and the oppression among her people."

Since on the law of averages, wisdom is productive of wealth, which has been taken to an extreme by the prosperity gospel, it is well to remember that there are many sayings where the sequence of cause - consequence are reversed for a time. Waltke argues:

> "since for a season the moral world may appear topsy-turvy, material wealth is not invariably the result of divine blessing, nor is poverty intrinsically the result of divine disfavor. Eventually, however, since the Lord upholds the moral order, the world must be righted so that the righteous are rewarded with material gain, and the wicked with material loss in a future that outlasts death" (*Proverbs*, vol. 1, p. 627).

II. WEALTH IN THE OLD TESTAMENT

Where There is Love

The last 'better than' statement is found in Prov. 15:17: "Better is a meal of vegetables where there is love than a fattened calf with hatred." This is a contrast between a cheerful heart that has a continual feast despite experiencing oppression all their days and the "fattened calf with hatred". Outward circumstances with a loving heart are much to be preferred to the best circumstances accompanied by hatred.

The essence of these 'better than' sayings is that poverty with righteousness is to be preferred over wealth with wickedness.

The Bright Side of Wealth

Wisdom writers who worked with the idea that character influenced consequences nevertheless knew of exceptions to this principle:

> "On what grounds, then, could the sages so confidently assert the superiority of righteousness even though they were aware of righteous folk who suffered and of wicked folk who prospered? *In general,* the sages clearly believed that wise and righteous behavior did make life better and richer, though virtue did not guarantee those consequences. Conversely, injustice, sloth, and the like generally have bad consequences." R. Van Leeuwen, *Wealth and Poverty,* Hebrew Studies, vol. 33, 1992, p. 32.

Wealth is Given as a Means to Honor God.

Prov. 14:31b: "whoever is kind to the needy honors God." The root for the verb 'honor' means to be heavy, which means to regard highly, to give the highest worth and value to a person, perhaps as the commandment indicates to father and mother (Ex. 20:12), but preeminently to God. Giving in support of the gospel is a matter pure and simple of honoring God. That is our highest motive, not only for giving but for all aspects of service and witness. This principle was reiterated in I Sam. 2:29-30. Eli had sons who were wicked men; they had no regard for the Lord. At least two important comments were made by the writer. "The sins of the young men were very great in the Lord's sight" (I Sam. 2:17; 2:22). They treated the Lord's offering with contempt and lived immorally. "Why do you honor your sons more than me..?" (2:29). "Those who honor me I will honor, but those who despise me will be disdained" (2:30). The psalmist says that God is clothed with splendor (honor) and majesty, strength and glory (Ps. 96:6; 104:1; cf. John 5:41-44). By virtue of God as Creator and Redeemer, those created in his image and redeemed by his blood, give glory, honor and thanks to God who sits on the throne and bow down in worship before him. (Rev. 4:11; 5:12-13).

The blessings of wealth and health are to be enjoyed and bring creaturely joy and praise to God. "When you have eaten and are satisfied, praise the LORD your God for the good land he has given you." (Deut. 8:10):

> "Then I realized that it is good and proper for a man to eat and drink, and to find satisfaction in his toilsome labor...Moreover when God gives any man wealth and possessions, and *enables him to enjoy them*, to accept his lot and be happy in his work - this is a gift of God." Eccles. 5:18-19

Obviously these material blessings are not the primary gift. They may be called common grace blessings that come because of God's lavish creation. They cannot satisfy in any ultimate sense because of what is said in Eccles. 3:11, "he has also set eternity in the hearts of men", and also because of the unpleasant interruption of our enjoyment of them at death. D. Kidner calls these pleasures 'mitigations'! They are from the hand of God. They point to our transience and the time-conditioned nature of these blessings (See Eccles. 2:24-26).

As long as eternity (olam) is in our hearts and likely a part of the image of God, the comparison of our fleeting moments with the idea of the eternal will prevent any final satisfaction with the gifts of creation. Kidner writes that these simple joys:

> "keep reminding us that these modest pleasures are not goals to live for, but bonuses or consolations to be gratefully accepted". He described these gifts of creation as palliatives brightening the "few days of one's life, the vain life which he has given us 'under the sun.'" *The Wisdom of Proverbs, Job and Ecclesiastes*, p. 100.

Acknowledging the Lord as the Source of Our Wealth

The sources of wealth in the O.T. are God, diligent work and inheritance. The supreme temptation to the wealthy is to say to themselves, "'My power and the strength of my hands have produced this wealth for me'. But *remember* the LORD your God, for it is he who gives you the ability to produce wealth" (Deut. 8:17-18). To remember God is not a mental act but a moral act. When God said through Jeremiah, "My people have forgotten, me days without number" (Jer. 2:32), the context of the passage makes it clear that their creed had not changed but rather the way in which they lived in relation to Yahweh their covenant Lord, had. They did not respond to Yahweh's corrective attempts (2:30). They felt able to say "we are free to roam; we will come to you no more" (2:31). They were as skilled as prostitutes in pursing love relationships with other gods.

Acknowledging God as the giver of every good and perfect gift must lead to the rejection of the myriad of all other gods in our world. The reminders not to forget God are many (Deut. 8:11, 14, 19) and not without cause. The hymn writer wrote, "Prone to wander, Lord I feel it, prone to leave the God I love". The source of our forgetfulness is given in 8:14. It is pride that leads to forgetfulness. Pride *excludes* from salvation. God opposes the proud but gives grace to the humble (Prov. 3:34, quoted in James 4:6 and I Peter 5:5). To see God's implacable opposition to pride one can do no better than to consult Isa. 2:6-22. Pride also seems to *exclude* from ministry. The story of Gideon and the Midianites is enlightening on this point. Gideon's army was reduced before the battle from twenty thousand to three hundred (Judg. 7:1-6). God's explanation to Gideon for this procedure was, "You have too many men for me to deliver Midian into their hands" (vs. 1). Several tests of the men were devised, "In order that Israel may not boast against me that her own strength has saved her" (vs. 2).

The O.T. praises diligence in work (Prov. 10:4-5; 13:4) as one of the sources of wealth and at the same time it is "the blessing of the LORD" which "brings wealth and he adds no trouble with it" (Prov. 10:22). The God who gives us ability expects us to use that ability and to work hard and to acknowledge him as its source. The Deut. text and indeed the whole of scripture rule out all suggestions that it is our hard work *alone*, apart from our God-given abilities that should receive the credit. As Wright says:

> "Self-exaltation and self-interest underlie the claim... 'I made it so I own it' is never the bottom line of biblical economics. The fact is that all hu-

man strength, gifts, abilities and life itself, along with the material resources out of which the wealth has been created, are the gifts of God. We are as little the makers of our own strength as we are the makers of the earth." *Deuteronomy, New International Biblical Commentary*, p. 128.

Helping the less fortunate is godly spending of wealth. Graciousness to the poor and needy honors the Lord (Prov. 14:31). Kindness to the poor is seen as "lending to the LORD" and such persons will be rewarded (Prov. 19:17). Those who are generous to the poor in sharing food with them will be blessed. The biblical imperative of compassion and common welfare must be taken seriously.

III. The Prosperity Gospel

Some preachers of the prosperity gospel have used selective portions of the O.T. to promulgate a message which argues that God has promised believers 'the good life' of material well-being, i.e. health, wealth and success. We will examine some of these arguments.

There are isolated texts, particularly in the O.T. which appear to support that position, as is the case in many other theological controversies. These texts tend to favor the view that God desires to lavish wealth on as many as will receive it in faith. They include Ps. 34:10; 35:27 and Josh. 1:8, which promise that meditating on the word of God will lead to his people making their way prosperous and being successful. Many argue that this presupposes universal laws governing health and wealth. The curses of the covenant, mentioned in Deut. 28:15-68, which include judgments concerning sickness, poverty and death are done away because "Christ redeemed us from the curse of the law by becoming a curse for us" (Gal. 3:13). It is claimed that since O.T. saints such as Abraham were promised the blessings of the covenant which included wealth then N.T. believers inherit these material promises, since they are the "children of Abraham" (Gal. 3:7) and "heirs according to the promise" to Abraham (Gal. 3:29). Deut. in particular, is said to teach that the rewards of obedience are spiritual and material. Although both Deut. and Prov. promise material and spiritual blessings, it is problematic to claim O.T. material blessings as gospel for today. These two books, although they promise material blessing at times without qualification, are dealing with the *collective* well-being of the nation of Israel, not of individuals.

Several additional problems arise with this twist on the gospel. Ethical decisions to obey God in the O.T. are not made on the basis of promises (to the nation or the individual) of personal well-being alone. O.T. ethics, which includes the gaining of wealth and its godly use, is based on the character of God. Practically speaking, doing the right thing in everyday life situations is the O.T.'s teaching on holiness, which impacts all aspects of life. Results do not influence what is right; it is the holy character of God and what he says that is of paramount importance.

Proverbs in particular is said to make a clear connection between wisdom, obedience and success, as defined by wealth. Key to this misunderstanding of what Prov. promises (or does not promise) is the word *hayim* (life). This noun is used thirty three times. Prov. 10:16: "The wages of the righteous bring them life, but the income of the wicked brings them punishment." Kidner comments:

> "In several places it is not too much to say that 'life' means fellowship with God…Some of the major Old Testament expressions for godliness are interchangeable with 'life' or 'to live'". *Proverbs,* O.T. TC, p. 3.

Life means essentially a relationship with God. Waltke concurs with Kidner's interpretation:

> "In sum, 'life', in the majority of Proverbs texts refers to abundant life in fellowship with God, a living relationship that is never envisioned as ending in clinical death in contrast to the wicked's eternal death." *Proverbs,* vol. 1, p. 105.

III. THE PROSPERITY GOSPEL

Now the significance of these quotes is to establish that the purpose of the book of Proverbs is not to draw a conclusion that wisdom will bring wealth as its principal purpose. As Kaiser says:

> "Since all of life is proclaimed as a 'gift' material benefits were regarded as no greater inducement than was life itself. Nor were material blessings of life looked upon as being greater in value than the rewards of wisdom and life themselves. It is a distinctively twentieth century obsession that fixes so singularly on the material aspects of life. The O.T. writers recommended that humans fix their eyes on 'the fear of the Lord" as the beginning point for all greatness and wealth (see e.g. Prov. 1:7)." *The Old Testament Promise of Material Blessings...*, p. 158.

Material well-being in the O.T. is to be a sign which confirms the corporate covenant with Israel (Deut. 8:18b). The blessings that confirm the covenant as a special relationship between God and Israel were a means of teaching the nations about Israel's special status. The visit of the queen of Sheba to Solomon in I Kings 10, exemplifies this. She had heard of Solomon's fame (vs. 1). Before she returned she said:

> "The report I heard in my own country about your achievements and your wisdom is true. But I did not believe these things until I came and saw with my own eyes. Indeed, not even half was told me; in *wisdom* and *wealth* you have far exceeded the report I heard."

With the Israelite theocracy currently shelved, at least temporarily, these statements that appear to suggest wealth

31

as an ironclad promise for the individual simply cannot be applied in the N.T. period.

Proverbs speaks both of the blessings of wealth and of the curse of wealth obtained amorally and illegally:

> "Proverbs consistently insists that righteousness outweighs wealth, and wickedness renders wealth worthless. Wealth which may appear as a blessing of the Creator is not intrinsically and invariably good. That depends on whether wealth is subordinate to righteousness, justice and wisdom." R. Van Leeuwen, *Wealth and Poverty in Proverbs*, Hebrew Studies, 1992, p. 31.

Of the many references to wealth in Proverbs some instruct youth to prize it (12:27) while a significant number instruct the youth not to trust it (11:28).

The book of Proverbs describes the benefits *and* the dangers of wealth. To read the positive texts and ignore the negative is an inadmissible procedure in biblical interpretation. Waltke makes several points in arguing for dealing with both sides of this question. It can easily be established that the promises of well-being are connected to the moral requirements of God's character and laws. They are not ironclad promises:

> "The sober, not the drunkard (cf. 23:29-35), the cool-tempered, not the hothead (15:18; 19:19; 22:24; 29:22), and the diligent, not the sluggard (see pp. 114-115) usually experience health and wealth." Waltke, *Proverbs*, p. 108.

Proverbs which seem to stand by themselves often do not and are qualified by what is seen to be a counterpoint.

III. THE PROSPERITY GOSPEL

Voices in counterpoint is a characteristic of the book of Proverbs, as Waltke notes:

> "The epigrammatic nature of the proverbs often causes the audience to overlook the counter proverbs that qualify these promises." *Proverbs*, vol. 1, p. 108

Such a counterpoint is exemplified by Prov. 26:4-5:

> "Do not answer a fool according to his folly, or you will be like him yourself." (vs. 4).
> "Answer a fool according to his folly, or he will be wise in his own eyes." (vs. 5).

In this case the counter-theme nature of Proverbs cannot be missed, but some individual proverbs are scattered throughout the book in no apparent order. In Other words there are qualifying proverbs that give us the full picture concerning wealth. If these are not taken into account wrong interpretations about the subject can easily be made.

The four 'better than' wealth statements certainly gainsay those who believe that the Bible teaches it is God's universal will for believers to be the recipients of his lavish gifts of financial well-being and success. The absolute, basic rules for life are wisdom, justice and righteousness. These rules trump any statements which appear to absolutize the promise of wealth. The prayer of Agur in 30:8-9, where he pleads with God requesting neither wealth nor poverty, cannot be reconciled with the gospel of affluence. The down drag of wealth and the power of temptation to cause the wealthy to forget and disown God is an insurmountable argument against the prosperity gospel. With these dangers to a believer why would God want all believers to be materially prosperous?

The prosperity gospel rests on several foundations which will come crumbling down when examined carefully of which the foremost is that God wants everyone to receive the wealth which is there for them if they claim it. What the Lord does want for every believer, without qualification, is to "Be holy, as I am holy" (Lev. 11:45; 19:2).

Wealth is not an end in itself, but a gracious gift from God to some to be used with a heart for God and his people's well-being. It is not to become an idol (Jer. 9:23-24). Wealth, to the extent that it was promised to the nation of Israel is inextricably bound up with covenant faithfulness. The earth is the Lord's (Ps. 24:1). The prosperity which flows from the created world is to be shared. The people of God in both testaments are to be stewards of God's good earth in the same way that the land was distributed to the various tribes, but it did not ultimately belong to them, since the Lord said, "The land is mine" (Lev. 25:23).

We have not attempted to deal with the prosperity gospel comprehensively or to look at it in the light of the New Testament. Kaiser combines both exegetical insights on key texts used by the prosperity gospel adherents with sound hermeneutical wisdom. He writes:

> "The prosperity gospel is a cultural captive of our affluent, success-crazy society. We recommend that we return to God's standards for success, prosperity, health and wealth. There are pieces of the truth in most of the claims made by those who espouse one aspect or another in the affluent gospel, but like most heresy, the false parts are accepted in the name of the small kernel of biblical truth found in each claim. What is needed is less proof-texting over random passages taken from here and there in the Scriptures. Instead, we need to develop large teaching passages on each of these themes and see what Scripture teaches in its wholeness, rather than

in just an assortment of bits and pieces." *"The O.T. Promise of Material Blessings and the Contemporary Believer"*, Trinity Journal, 9, New Series, p. 119.

To summarize, the prosperity gospel can not stand if we consider the O.T. evidence alone for the following reasons: First, if riches can be claimed by faith in the O.T. promises of wealth and success, why are there serious warning in the O.T. against trusting in wealth or making wealth a focus in one's life? The focus is one-sided if wealth is emphasized. What Proverbs is centered on is *life* which as we have seen refers to fellowship with God. Second, there are promises that God will meet our needs, but needs and wants are two different things. In the light of the N.T. we should have contentment in life if food and clothing are ours. Third, the preoccupation with wealth as needed and promised by God, if claimed by faith, ignores the many inherent dangers spelled out in the O.T. in possessing wealth. Fourth, the focus in Proverbs and Other O.T. books is not primarily on promises wealth or success but on the call to live life in the fear of the Lord. For a powerful critique of this perspective from the N.T., see John Piper's Newsletter *Prosperity Preaching: deceitful and deadly*, Feb14, 2007 and also Gordon Fee, *The Disease of the Health and Wealth Gospel*.

IV. Jesus and Wealth

In Luke 16:11 worldly wealth is contrasted with true riches. Jesus said, "So if you have not been trustworthy in handling worldly wealth, who will trust you with true riches?" Worldly wealth is probably to be understood as wealth that is earned unjustly or wealth used exclusively or primarily for self, or that becomes an idol. True riches are best understood as our relationship with God. Only grace is men and women's lasting possession. The O.T. also contains many verses describing this contrast between false ideas of what wealth is or can do. One such is Prov. 11:4: "Wealth is worthless in the day of wrath, but righteousness delivers from death."

Jesus spoke of the ultimate worthlessness of wealth when he said, "What good will it be for a man if he gains the whole world, yet forfeits his soul?" (Matt. 16:26). In the parable of Luke 12:13-21, Jesus was confronted with two brothers fighting over an inheritance. Jesus took the occasion to speak of greed: "A man's life does not consist in the abundance of his possessions" (vs. 15). He then told the story of a business man who built bigger and bigger barns so he would be prepared when his business expanded. But there is no indication that the rich man (vs. 16) gained his wealth illegally or was engaged in any sordid deal, nor that he was oppressing the poor (as in Micah 2:2-4 or Amos 8). Jesus simply points out a reality that many do not want to face, i.e. death (vs. 20), and the final statement is the most probing of all. "This is how it will be (as he universal izes the message) with anyone (not limited to the wealthy) who stores up things for himself but *is not rich toward God*" (vs. 21).

Notice that in the story which Jesus told about building bigger barns that God said to him, "You fool" (vs. 20). There are many references to a fool in Proverbs and in the Psalms (Ps. 14:1). One of the terms describes the fool as a person rejecting the fear of the Lord. The fool is not mentally deficient but spiritually unwilling to receive any instruction which comes from anywhere outside himself. "They hated knowledge and did not choose to fear the LORD" (Prov. 1:29).

Luke 16 is one of the best known stories, about a rich man and Lazarus, a beggar. It must first be said that the rich man was not lost because he was rich, nor was the poor man saved because he was poor. The rich man was lost because he was totally self-centered and oblivious to the beggar at his front door. His wealth blinded him to others and their needs. Giving to the poor is contrasted with the one who closes his eyes to them and who will receive many curses (Prov. 28:27b). The rich man may have thought that the poor man was getting what he deserved but in so doing he was "mocking the poor and showing contempt for their maker" (Prov. 17:5).

Matthew 19:16-20; Mark 10:17 -31; Lk.18:18-29.

In these passages Jesus is asked an extremely important question recorded by all three synoptic gospels - the question "Good teacher, what must I do to inherit eternal life?" Luke tells us the man was a ruler, and Mark describes him as running up to Jesus and kneeling before him (10:17). That he was asking what he must do to gain eternal life is to his credit. He was looking for something beyond what could be found in the present world. Some never ask this important question, particularly if their vision is clouded by riches. Jesus spoke elsewhere (Matt. 13:22) of the "worries of this life and the deceitfulness of wealth" as that which "chokes" the message of the gospel.

Is it significant that he addressed Jesus as "good"? Jesus' cryptic reply first addresses the word 'good'. "Why do you call me good? No one is good but God alone" (Mark 10:18; Luke 18:19). Moreover, Jesus points the man to the commandments to highlight that only God defines what is good (Deut. 10:13). "He has showed you, O man, what is good" (Micah 6:8). Jesus wants the rich young ruler to reflect upon what he has just said. If he addressed Jesus as good and if only God was good, as the rabbis taught, then this young man was declaring something important about Jesus. The young man is not merely speaking with an average Jewish rabbi. . Jesus is showing the man not only that good has been revealed by God, but suggesting that his connection with God is not limited to his being a teacher. Jesus is showing the rich young ruler that Jesus, as Messiah, is uniquely identified with God

When asked a similar question, "What must we do to do the works God requires?" Jesus replied, "The work of God is this: to believe in the one he has sent." (John 6:28-29). In this instance rather than point to the works of the law, Jesus points to an act of faith. Why not so with the rich young ruler? Jesus knows the heart and knows what each individual needs to see before he can come to Christ. The rich young ruler may not have seen himself as a sinner. Jesus points him to the commandments and instructs him to keep them (Mark 10:19) in order that these might reveal to him that he was a sinner (cf. Rom 7:7-8) and that eternal life which the man sought, is a gift from God to those who see that by their own efforts it cannot be attained.

The young man responds that he had kept the commandments from the time he was a boy (vs. 20). Had he, or was he blinded by pharisaical legalism which saw the commandments as exclusively dealing with externals and not the heart? We must assume that he was sincere in believing that he had kept the law; but sincerely wrong.

The commandments to which Jesus referred the young man were from the second half of the Decalogue. These are commandments that deal with one's personal relationships and attitudes towards others. Jesus placed the command-ment to obey our parents at the end rather than at the beginning of the last six. Was he doing so to draw attention to it? Jesus was concerned about violations of this commandment (Matt. 15:1-6; Mark 7:9-13). Had the rich young ruler violated the spiritual intent of this law of God as understood or expounded by Jesus in the Sermon on the Mount? Perhaps he was selfish, prompting Jesus to confront him on this issue, urging him to sell all and give to the poor and amass heavenly treasure:

> "'one thing you lack. Go, sell everything you have and give to the poor and you will have treasure in heaven. Then come follow me'. At this the man's face fell. He went away sad, because he had great wealth." Mark 10:21-22.

Jesus went directly to this individual's particular prob-lem: he was a sinner, and was wedded to his riches, he loved his wealth more than people. The young ruler's response was to go away sad from Jesus presence. His wealth held him back from the kingdom of God. Con-fronted with the choice given him by Jesus, he chose his wealth over the Savior. And yet, "Jesus loved him" (vs. 21a). Jesus' warnings (rebuke) throughout the gospels about the potential destructive power of riches are evidence of his love. Comfort (Rom. 15:4) and rebuke (II Tim. 3:16) are both parts of the purposes of scripture. The God who loves also warns those that he loves.

IV. JESUS AND WEALTH

Jesus' counsel in this instance is not to be taken as a universal principle in scripture. It was particular to the young man's situation and need. We are not all proven to be sinners by violation of the same commandment.

However, when we come to Christ the principle of giving up 'all' for Jesus, is not necessarily restricted to money (Luke 14:33). How does the prosperity gospel, which accentuates the human desire for wealth, fit with Jesus' statement concerning the extreme difficulty of the rich to enter the kingdom of God? James speaks of the wrong kind of friendship (friendship with the world), which causes one to be an enemy of God (James 4:4). This is a cozying-up to the Jesus-hating world, living its values, values that are antithetical to God's. What a lesson for the disciples and for us!

Jesus goes on to draw a rather severe conclusion about "How hard it is for the rich to enter the kingdom of God!" (Matt. 19:23-24; Mark 10:23; Luke 18:24-25). The disciples, were astonished at hearing this (Mark 10:26), probably because of the assumed connection between piety and wealth and since all things in life are easier for the rich, attaining heaven must be the same. However, that understanding was unfortunately incorrect, as books such as Ecclesiastes, Proverbs, Psalm 49 and Job make clear. Wealth creates an aura of false independence (Rev. 3:17). It leads one to think anything can be bought and that one can get whatever is desired. The wealthy think they can buy themselves into happiness and buy themselves out of sorrow and difficulties in life. Why would this type of person think God was needed? Wealth tends to shackle a person to this world. "For where your treasure is, there will your heart be also" (Matt. 6:21). If this world occupies our exclusive attention and interest, what is the role of the world to come? Material possessions tend to limit our vision of the importance of eternity and of heavenly treasures or true riches. There is a saying, "For a hundred people who can stand adversity only one can stand prosperity." When touring a magnificent estate, Dr. Johnson was said to remark, "these are the things which make it difficult to die." Wealth may cause one to ignore the needed perspective of the apostle Paul "So we fix our eyes, not on what is seen, but on what is unseen. For what is seen is temporary, but what is unseen is eternal" (II Cor. 4:18).

All who come to Christ give up their self-importance and self-sufficiency to follow him. "Small is the gate and narrow the road that leads to life and only a few find it" (Matt. 7:14).

When Jesus declared that it was "hard ... for the rich to enter the kingdom of God!" the word 'hard' must be taken seriously but does not mean 'impossible for God'. Jesus illustrated in pictorial form the degree of how hard it was for the rich to enter the kingdom of God. He followed his statement in Mark 10:24 with a bit of humor and hyperbole to make his point. He did the same in his reference to the "speck of sawdust in your brother's eye" and the "plank in your own" (Matt. 7:3-5). While the eye of a needle is sometimes believed to refer to a tiny gate for entering the city such cannot be proven. Since Jesus went on to talk about the human impossibility of reaching the rich for the kingdom of God, likewise it is impossible for a camel to go through the eye of a needle. This is the language of hyperbole which drives home the lesson: it is humanly impossible for the rich to enter the Kingdom of God. But God's grace can reach the heart of the rich and change it so that their attachment to worldly riches will give way to a new attachment to the true riches which Jesus often talked about (Luke 16:11).

Jesus response to the disciple's question, "Well then, who can be saved?" is good news for all but especially for the rich whose hearts can be changed by the power of the gospel. "With man, this is impossible, but not with God; all things are possible with God (Mark 10:27). If it is hard for the rich, is it not hard for us as well, since, in many respects, we are rich? When Jesus said it was difficult he continued to say that with humans it was impossible, but God can overcome the difficulty and will make the impossible possible (See I Cor.1:25-27).

The demand to the rich young ruler to give up earthly comfort requires all of us to see the seriousness with which Jesus viewed the dangerous influence of wealth.

Mark 12:41-44

There is a small but instructive story in Mark's gospel about Jesus observing rich and poor as they put their money in the temple treasury. Jesus "watched the crowd" (12:41) as they gave. I wonder how church giving would be influenced if we were conscious that Jesus was watching. Some do not like that thought because it conjures up for them the notion of a God who is anxious to catch us in our failures. However, that incident evoked one of Jesus' most important sayings on giving. This story in Mark 12: 41-44 is preceded in the gospel by Jesus' scathing attack on religious hypocrisy (vs. 38-40). The outwardly religious like ceremonies where they can wear long robes and be seen. They love to be regarded as pious and to be greeted in the market place and have the highly prominent seats at banquets and the places of honor in the synagogues. They major in the externals but "they devour widows' houses and for a show make lengthy prayers" (vs. 40). This preceding context is significant in contrasting external displays of religious behavior with the simple loving devotion of a widow! It is a human foible to concentrate on the outward appearance when we know that God examines the heart (I Sam.16:7).

As the story unfolds, rich and poor were noticed by Jesus and the rich were contributing "large amounts" (vs. 41).

The widow reached into her purse and put in two small coins which amounted to only a smaller portion of a cent. It is this remarkable situation which Jesus used as a teaching lesson when he precedes it with his customary emphatic phrase, "I tell you the truth". It must have started the disciples to hear Jesus say that her contribution exceeded all the others (vs. 43). The point is driven home to the disciples. The rich gave out of their wealth. The widow gave out of her poverty (vs. 44) and that was all she had to live on.

How could Jesus have said that the woman gave more (vs. 42)? Jesus' math is based not on the quantitative amount but on the proportional nature of the gift. They gave a lot and had a lot left over. She gave a miniscule amount but was destitute after.

This story must have resonated during the early apostolic period and led to the apostles coming up with a system for caring for widows (Acts 6:1-3; I Tim. 5:3-6). Jesus is establishing the principle of sacrificial, proportionate giving where what is left after we give must come into consideration as well as the amount actually given (tithe or anything beyond it). The rich in their responses are perhaps being held prisoner by their money. The widow demonstrated that she was not a captive to her money.

V. Paul and Wealth

I Corinthians 16:1-4

Here Paul is speaking about a collection of money which was to be taken to the Jewish believers in Jerusalem who were poor due to their suffering oppression. Paul mentions this collection in Rom. 15:25-27 and we see from vs. 27 at least part of Paul's motivation for doing this. "For if the Gentiles have shared in the Jews' spiritual blessings, they owe it to the Jews to share with them their material blessings" (Rom. 15:27). Based on II Cor. 8:13-14, Paul saw this giving to the Jerusalem poor as an expression of Christian unity. This had been on Paul's heart for some time.

In writing his second letter to the Corinthians Paul speaks of their sacrificial giving as an act of "obedience that accompanies your confession of the gospel of Christ" (9:13). It was an act of generosity in sharing with the needy in Jerusalem. It will be reciprocated by the saints in Jerusalem, not with money, but with "prayers for you … because of the surpassing grace God has given you" (II Cor. 9:13-14).

Paul had laid this matter before the church the previous year (II Cor.8:10). They responded by initially giving, though the gift was not sent at that time. Paul speaks of their *eager willingness* to complete the project (8:11). They may have set aside some money but they needed to do so on a regular and systematic basis, so that when Paul came again the funds would be available to be carried to Jerusalem.

How did Paul want them to respond? He had a plan. The community at Corinth was meeting on the first day of the week. This was the day of worship based on the resurrection of Christ. The Corinthians were to "set aside a sum of money in keeping with" their "income, saving it up" until Paul arrived. Note that it was to be proportionate to income (I Cor. 16:2). This systematic saving plan of Paul's was so that when he came there would be no financial crisis. The goal would have been arrived at over many weeks by their regular and systematic giving.

Although there was a synagogue in the city these Gentile believers would not have had biblical teaching or godly models on the subject. If Paul had a percentage in mind to be given, he did not specify it. Had he wished, he could have fallen back on the O.T. tithe, but he did not. Arguments from silence are always problematic but if Paul wanted to specify the tithe this would have been a good time and place say so. It was left to the individual family to look at their circumstances and out of gratitude and hearts of love, to give as God had prospered them. It was to be what one writer has called, "a carefully designed program of stewardship" G. Getz, *A Biblical Theology of Material Possessions*, p. 209. Paul was not giving an absolute methodology.

II Corinthians 8 & 9 - Heavenly Value of Earthly Gifts

1. Giving is an act of grace, especially when performed with generosity under severely adverse circumstances, not grudgingly but with joyfulness, according to ability and beyond (II Cor. 8:1-4, 6-7b; 9:5).

2. Giving is at their own initiative, a service to the saints, an extension of themselves, not mechanical but the outworking of our relationship with God (II Cor. 8:3-4).
3. Giving was first to the Lord and then to the church in Jerusalem; not simply an act of charity but of devotion and worship - the result of an enlightened view of the cross (II Cor. 8:5, 9; 9:15).
4. Giving is a grace to be sought and to excel at as part of a full and complete Christian experience (II Cor. 8:7).
5. Giving is an expression of Christian unity and fellowship (II Cor. 8:5, 13-14).
6. Giving is an expression of Christian equality through sharing, a test of sincerity (II Cor. 8:8).
7. Giving is incarnational and modeled after Christ's example; his indescribable gift on the cross is its basis (II Cor. 8:9; 9:15).
8. Giving is according to means, not only a desire but a performance (II Cor. 8:11-12).
9. Human need teaches mutual dependence; supporting those in need honors the Lord. (II Cor. 8:14-15, 19).
10. Giving is proof of love and a source of satisfaction, beneficial to other churches when done in a way proper in God's eyes (II Cor. 8:19-21).
11. Giving is not a response to human pressure but to holy persuasion, spontaneous and with joy, decided on before the Lord (II Cor. 9:7).
12. Giving is an act of righteousness which produces a harvest that enables continued generosity (II Cor. 9:10).
13. Giving is an act of obedience accompanying confession of the gospel which results in praise going to the Lord (II Cor. 9:11-13).
14. The beneficiaries of your gifts pray for you and are bonded in love toward you because of the surpassing grace given to you (II Cor. 9:14).

I Timothy 6:6-10, 17-19

In his letter to Timothy, Paul reminds us of truths which we earlier encountered in the O.T. Even in the apostolic days Paul had to argue against those "who think that godliness is a means to financial gain" (I Tim. 6:5b). Earlier in that letter he had encouraged elders "not to be a lover of money" (3:3). Some teachers apparently put on a mask to cover up greed, but not Paul:

> "Probably these false teachers have picked up (I Thes. 2:5) some clues from the culture and are teaching to curry people's favor and eventually their money". G. Fee, *1 & 2 Timothy, Titus*, New International Bible Commentary, p. 142. see also Titus 1:11.

If we are focused on wealth, the earthly treasure blocks our vision of the heavenly treasure (Matt. 6:19). This is an uncomfortable message but a necessary one for all of us, particularly those living in the west, inundated with materialistic visions of what is most vital. Materialism is already a problem in the churches of the developing world. Paul's focus in the Timothy passage is on *contentment*, which he says comes when we are satisfied with food and clothing (6:8). "We brought nothing into the world, and we can take nothing out of it" (vs. 7). This is very similar to the sentiment which Job expressed in 1:21. Paul's statement that we can take nothing out of it, rules out the frantic obsession with more and more which is inconsistent with the N.T. teaching on contentment. There may be some similarities to the teaching of the Stoics, but in his remarks Paul gives an allusion to the O.T. text (vs. 7; Eccles.5:15) followed by one to the teaching of Jesus (vs. 8; cf. Luke 12:15).

V. PAUL AND WEALTH

I Timothy 6:6-10 - Dangers of wealth

This passage is a clear warning against those "who want to get rich" (vs. 9). Since vs. 10 speaks of the "love of money is a root of all kinds of evil" and that some people are "eager for money" it is likely that Paul's admonition concerning those who "want to get rich" refers to the excessive, greedy wanting into which some have fallen. Paul has made one of the qualifications of a spiritual leader to be "not a lover of money" (I Tim. 3:3), i.e. not to use the ministry for financial gain.

Although Paul probably had some false teachers in mind in these ethical exhortations, these words apply to all Christians because they are consistent with what Jesus taught about wealth. An unhealthy desire for wealth results in the following:

1. Falling "into temptation"
2. "and a trap"
3. "and into many foolish and harmful desires"
4. "that plunge men into ruin and destruction" (vs. 9)
5. "the love of money is a root of all kinds of evil" (vs. 10).

On this point, Fee remarks that:

> "Paul's point is not theological precision on the relationship of greed to all other sins." G. Fee, *I & II Timothy, Titus*, p. 145.

And Calvin continues:

> "There is no need to be too careful in comparing other vices with this. It is true that ambition and pride often bring forth worse fruits, and yet ambition does not spring from covetousness. The same is

true of sexual lusts. But Paul did not intent to include under covetousness every kind of vice we can
name." New Testament Commentaries, *The First
and Second Epistles of Paul to Timothy*, p. 275.

6. and causes some to wander from the faith,
7. by which they pierce "themselves with many griefs"
   (vs. 10).

It is difficult for contemporary Christians to take these
warnings seriously. The story is told of one of John Wesley's followers coming to him rejoicing over an inheritance
he had received. Wesley's response was, "We will pray for
you". The desires of vs. 9 are called *foolish* because they
cannot bring any ultimate good into one's life; they are called *harmful* because they may cause someone to "wander
from the faith" and to "engage in all kinds of evil" and
"pierce themselves with many griefs". Wealth can be used
for the well-being of others and for the glory of God. Yet
there are spiritual dangers in it as is clear from the word
"trap" (vs. 9) which may refer to a trap set by the Evil One.
He certainly employed the allure of power and wealth in
the temptation of Jesus (Matt. 4:8-11).

These warnings about the potential danger to one's
spiritual life were first issued in the O.T. "Do not wear
yourself out to get rich" (Prov. 23:4a). "Death and Destruction are never satisfied, and neither are the eyes of
man" (Prov. 27:20). Scripture uses the eyes to point to men
and women's lust for illegitimate desires (Gen. 3:6-7). "I
denied myself nothing my eyes desired; I refused my heart
no pleasure" (Eccles. 2:10; cf. 1:8). "There was no end to
his toil, yet his eyes were not content with his wealth"
(Eccles. 4:8). "A faithful man will be richly blessed, but
one eager to get rich will not go unpunished" (Prov. 28:20).
These sentiments are also expressed in Eccles. 5:10: "Who-

soever loves money never has money enough; whoever loves wealth is never satisfied with his income".

I Timothy 6:17-19- A Godly Use of Wealth

Paul moves from instruction about the negative possibilities and potential dangers facing the rich (6:6-10), to positive instructions to the rich about what to do with their wealth. His first command is for the rich not to be arrogant (vs. 17). Wealth gives one power and is often attended by pride. Prov. 10:15 tells us that the rich find their security not in God but in their wealth which they regard as "their fortified city". Such a city is surrounded by high walls that will protect from all forces of danger. Wealth is here seen falsely to be their guardian and protector "they imagine their wealth an unscaleable wall" (Prov. 18:11b). Safety is not in their wealth, as the preceding verse makes clear: "The name of the Lord is a strong tower; the righteous run to it and are safe" (Prov. 18:10).

Riches are "uncertain" (I Tim. 6:17) because they are *given by God* and for sufficient reasons may be taken away. Such was the case with Job and was true in the life of Joseph. It may be so, but Paul is contrasting riches in the present period with the laying up of "treasure for themselves as a firm foundation *for the coming age*" (6:19). The rich are to put their hope in God not in wealth. They are commanded to do good and to be rich in good deeds, to be generous and willing to share (6:18). Riches used in the interest of the kingdom of God provide the wealthy with opportunity for doing good which may not be available to others of a more meager income, yet Paul tells *everyone*, both rich and poor, as a result of Christ's saving death to be "eager to do what is good" (Tit. 2:14b).

Enjoyment does not mean to indulge oneself to the fullest. We are not to live for pleasure (I Tim. 5:6), certainly not when we substitute pleasure for God. Tragically we are living in a period of time in the history of God's people when all around us and sometimes within the church we are warned against being

> "lovers of themselves, lovers of money, ... not lovers of the good, ... lovers of pleasure rather than lovers of God - having a form of godliness but denying its power" (2 Tim. 3:1-5).

Paul has a balanced view of riches and poverty. If in the providence of God and through hard work and the blessing of the Lord one becomes rich, thankfulness to God and generosity to the causes of God in the world are to be pursued. God's program incorporates the proclamation of the gospel and the care of the disadvantaged in the world.

VI. Comparisons between the Testaments

The motive for giving in the O.T. was gratefulness for Yahweh's covenant love and a desire to obey him in all that was commanded, including the principles of regulated giving. The level of the experience of what the truth required was connected with the amount of the truth revealed at various stages of divine revelation. Since the truth revealed in the O.T. was awaiting the fullness of revelation and redemption in the N.T., we may expect some differences in the matter of giving between the testaments.

There are more specific comments emphasizing the internal attitudes toward giving in the N.T. Joy and sacrifice, and liberality and thankfulness, in the use of our wealth quite naturally are related to the gift of grace in the cross of Jesus Christ. Naturally the fullness of God's revealed truth became a greater reality in his Son who had now come in the fullness of time (Gal. 4:4-5). God's indescribable gift of Christ (II Cor. 9:15) and Christ's grace in becoming poor so that we could become rich (II Cor. 8:9) move us to give far beyond what the O.T. law on tithing could do.

So often the apostle spoke of giving as a grace (subjective) (II Cor. 8:1, 6, 7b). The gospel both saves and sanctifies. It teaches us not to "conform any longer to the pattern of this world, but be transformed by the renewing of your minds" (Rom. 12:2a). It is to be expected that believers in the new covenant period will operate with greater resources and abilities to do what God has said than in the O.T. Indeed this was the promise made in the new covenant passages in Jer. 31:31-34, where the prophet says "I (God) will put my law in their minds and write it on their hearts" (vs. 33) as also in 32:39-40 and Ezek. 36:27. "I will put my Spirit in you and move you to follow my decrees and be careful to keep my laws".

There was a certain emphasis in the old covenant on giving *willingly* to the Lord (Exod. 25:2; I Chron. 28:9; Ezra 6:6). Yet Christ's person and work is no longer seen in the shadow of the O.T. revelation but now in the full blaze of the N.T. revelation. We who live after the Christ event have been given greater resources and abilities (Matt. 11:11; 13:16-17; I Pet.1:12) to respond to the demands of love, since love enables before it commands. In the new covenant Paul commends the Corinthians for giving "beyond their ability" and says that they "urgently pleaded with us for the privilege of sharing in this service to the saints" (II Cor. 8:3-4). "God so loved the world that he gave … (John 3:16). New covenant love has the advantage over the old covenant. "A new commandment I give you: Love one another. *As I have loved you,* so you must love one another" (John. 13:34).

The Old Testament Tithe - Valid for Today?

In speaking of wealth in both testaments we are led to the question of the O.T. tithe and its validity for today. Christian thinking is not agreed on this subject. Some believers are strongly of the opinion that churches should be urging people to tithe. Yet if the tithing law of the O.T. were to continue, one would expect some mention of it in major teaching passages on giving in the N.T. or on the lips of Jesus. In addition the question of the tithe and its continuation in the N.T. hangs on the question whether the tithing laws were part of the *moral law* which continues into the N.T. or the *ceremonial law* which does not. Sometimes appeal is made to the references in the patriarchal period of Abraham and Jacob paying tithes. (Gen. 14:20; 28:22). Abraham gave a tenth of the booty of war but there is no evidence that such a practice continued. Jacob's reference to the tenth occurs in a context in which he seems to be bargaining with God. The tithe in the Mosaic Law was compulsory; the N.T. does not see giving as a compulsory act. II Cor. 8:3-4 emphasizes giving as a free will response. The tithe was also accompanied by the offerings. The two cannot be separated from each other. When Malachi accused the nation of robbing God and was asked, "How do we rob God?" his answer was "In tithes and offerings" (Mal. 3:8).

Since the two belong together both in terms of their roles in supporting temple worship and those who serve there and in form, i.e. agricultural products, if tithes are deemed obligatory, then the same must be said concerning the offerings. Pieter Verhoef convincingly argued that the Hebrew word for 'offering', in the phrase "tithes and offerings" is unquestionably part of Israel's ceremonial law.

Some may feel that passages such as Matt. 23:23; Luke 11:42; and 18:12 point to the continuation of the tithe in the N.T. dispensation. These statements join with others which Jesus uttered at the time in his life prior to his death, when the ceremonial law was still operative. Matt. 15:24 is another example of a statement made by Jesus but only true in the light of the O.T. dispensation which was present until Jesus accomplished his redemptive mission at Calvary. The O.T. covenant was in force until Jesus' death (Heb. 9:15-17). Prior to his death Jesus followed the O.T. ceremonies in the law though somewhat more loosely than the Pharisees. The statements which Jesus made concerning tithing were normative for the O.T. dispensation but not the N.T. It

might even be argued that Jesus' statements were contrasting the weightier matters of the law - justice, mercy
and faithfulness (Matt. 23:23), being the law's moral requirements, with the ceremonial stipulations (tithing mint,
dill and cumin) which were a part of the old dispensation.

This leads to the conclusion that the references which
Jesus made to the tithe do not support it as part of God's
universal moral law. Apostolic stipulations (I Cor. 16:2; II
Cor. 9:5) do not urge a legalistic routine for giving (I Cor.
16:2) but giving as a willing gift (II Cor. 8:3-5), out of love.

There are elements of continuity and discontinuity between the testaments in the realm of material giving. The
N.T. speaks of the ceremonial laws as 'shadows' of what is
to come in Christ (Col. 2:17; Heb.10:1). These laws point
to the new covenant order in Christ.

> "Moses was faithful as a servant in all God's house,
> testifying to what *would be said in the future*" (Heb.
> 3:5).

The Mosaic economy was typological of the spiritual
realities of the new covenant.

> ".. in connection with tithing, it must be clear that it
> belonged in conjunction with the whole system of
> giving and offering, to the dispensation of shadows
> and that it therefore has lost its significance as a
> *schema* of giving under the new covenant. In this
> respect we have both continuity and discontinuity.
> The continuity consists in the principle of giving,
> and the discontinuity in the obligation of giving in
> accordance to the *schema* of tithes….The law is in
> every respect a pointer to, and a prophecy of the
> new order of life, which only Christ can inaugu-
> rate." Verhoef, p. 127.

In the new covenant there is considerable emphasis that everything belongs to God. We are but stewards and we will give an account of how our wealth has been used one day.

There is an additional difficulty in catapulting the O.T. tithe into the N.T. The plural tithes is used in Mal. 3:8b and elsewhere in the O.T. There appear to be three tithes in the O.T. Thus to talk about tithing in the Mosaic dispensation we must realize that it was not a tenth but likely an aggregate minimum of 23%. The measure of giving in the O.T. cannot therefore be set at 10%.

Of course, even then we encounter several questions that those who see the tithe carrying into the N.T. cannot answer from scripture. Do we tithe the gross income or the net income? Given what the state takes today in the form of taxes, compare with O.T. times (see I Sam. 8:14), how should we take that into account? The N.T. statements on giving penetrate to the heart. These N.T. principles do not approach the question of *how much* with any kind of legalistic spirit.

In addition to those who speak of the tithe as the normative standard in the NT, there are two additional positions to be mentioned. Some would regard tithing as the secret of growing one's church. If that were true, there needs to be care that such does not lead to the unconscious and unarticulated thought that, after I give my tithe that is the end of the matter and now I can do pretty well as I please with the remainder. Addressing these questions at a ministers' conference in early 2004, quoting Jesus words in Mark 10: 23-27 and Paul's warning in I Tim. 6:9, John Piper pleaded:

> "Do we talk to our people this way? Or do we just want them to tithe? My take on tithing in America is that it's a middle-class way of robbing God. Tithing to the church and spending the rest on your family

is not a Christian goal. It's a diversion. The real issue is: How shall we use God's trust fund, namely, all we have, - for his glory? In a world with so much misery, what lifestyle should we call our people to live? What example are we setting?

I think the reason God ordains the use of money is so that we will use it to show that he is more precious than what money can buy. Money is one means of making much of God. It's a means of making visible the location of our heart: Where your treasure is...."

Somewhere between the position of the tithe as the standard of giving and Piper's remark that "tithing in America is a middle-class way of robbing God" is R. Sider's proposal for the graduated tithe: "A Modest Proposal for Christian Giving in a Starving World." Given the hold which wealth potentially has on the fallen human person, he writes:

"We have been brainwashed to believe that bigger houses, more prosperous businesses and more luxurious gadgets are worthy goals in life. As a result we are caught in an absurd materialistic spiral. The more we make, the more we think we need in order to live decently and respectfully." *The Enterprise,* winter 1961, reprinted in *Theology News and notes,* Oct 1975, Fuller Theological Seminary.

To break this vicious cycle he proposes the *graduated* tithe, which means the more you make after a certain base amount, the more you give. He suggests figuring out carefully and honestly what we would *need* for a year. Once that basic amount is arrived at (presupposing want is not interpreted as need), the tithe is given on that basic amount.

Each family's needs also takes account of the number of children in the family. Then for each $1,000 earned beyond that basic amount a gradual increase is made.

Sider is not pontificating on the percentage of increase after the basic amount. It is not a new legalism; his particular percentages are not radical. Obviously many other scales could be and are being developed. He advises:

> "Most of us will almost certainly need the support and guidance of other committed brothers and sisters if we are going to radically alter our affluent lifestyles....We must discover new ways to help each other in the body of Christ to adopt a lifestyle which is totally and unconditionally surrendered to the Lord of the poor" *The Enterprise,* winter 1961, reprinted in *Theology News and Notes,* Fuller Theological Seminary, Oct 1975.

VII. How Then Shall We Give?

We have seen the overwhelming biblical evidence of a bright side and a dark side to wealth. The bright side can be subsumed under the heading, 'how should our money be used?' The dark side is particularly important in the present age because we are inundated with the philosophy, at every practical level, that the 'good life' is the life focused on the pleasures of a materialistic world. It would seem that the original statements of the fall, particularly Gen.3:6-7 are being lived out with a vengeance today. As Christians we are not called to have a complex about earning money and becoming wealthy. We are called to take seriously Jesus' remarks about a spiritual treasure where moth and rust does not corrupt. There is a delicate tension with which a believer lives out his/her life in this matter. John Wesley's famous advice is still good advice: "Earn all you can, save all you can, give all you can". The gospel is intended to enable us to overcome our self-centeredness in all areas of life, in marriage as in this case, money.

To take the lessons on wealth in the old and new testaments to heart, a final question must be asked: Who are the rich in today's world? Unfortunately many today, despite several cars, house and cottage and every imaginable gadget for making life easier would be startled to think they are the rich. Of course the Bible does not give us annual income figures to determine if we are being addressed as rich in the biblical passages. Perhaps Paul's statement about food and clothing (which may include property) as the necessities with which we should be content, may provide at least a partial definition. Are middle class North Americans rich? Of course not if the comparison is with the entrepreneur who has made this year's list of billionaires. Our contemporary culture parades over the television "Life Styles of the Rich and Famous". Supposedly we are to be envious of such opulence. The true believer will not be overawed with these displays but will pay more attention to what Jesus and the rest of the N.T. says. There is no doubt that the world esteems wealth highly. However, on one occasion, when the Pharisees sneered at him (Luke 16:14), Jesus said, "You cannot serve both God and Money" (16:13), and went on to say "What is highly valued among men is detestable in God's sight" (16:15b). We must make a choice not to become captive to a secular materialistic culture. Christ, by his victorious and bloody death, has overcome the world (John 16:33). Regeneration gives the believer the power to overcome the world (I John 5:4; Rev.2:7). Because, as Christians we operate with an eternal perspective, we know that "The world and its desires pass away, but the man who does the will of God lives forever" (I John 2:17).

Some of the wisdom from the past may help us with this important issue:

> "How we use our money demonstrates the reality of our love for God. In some ways it proves our love more conclusively than depth of knowledge, length of prayers or prominence of service."
>
> Charles C. Ryrie

> "If a man's religion does not affect his use of money, that man's religion is vain."
>
> Hugh Martin

VII. HOW THEN SHALL WE GIVE?

"It is possible to love money without having it, and it is possible to have it without loving it."

"Money, in truth, is one of the most unsatisfying of possessions. It takes away some cares, no doubt; but it brings with it quite as many cares as it takes away. There is the trouble in the getting of it; anxiety in the keeping of it; temptations in the use of it; guilt in the abuse of it; sorrow in the losing of it and perplexity in the disposing of it."

Bishop J.C. Ryle

"There are two ways in which a Christian may view his money - 'How much of my money shall I use for God?' Or 'How much of God's money shall I use for myself?"

W. Graham Scroggie

"The love of money is a greater curse to the church than the aggregate of all the Other evils in the world."

Samuel Chadwick

"Time and money are the heaviest burdens of life, and the unhappiest of all mortals are those who have more of either than they know how to use."

Samuel Johnson

VIII. Study Questions

II. Wealth in the Old Testament

Deut. 8:1-18

1) Notice the bright and dark sides in this passage.
   a) In vs. 10 how should the blessing of wealth impact our lives?
   b) According to vss. 12-14, what is the source of temptation?
2) Look at the prayer in Prov. 30:7-9.
   a) Note the similarity to the prayer in Deut. 8:12-14.
   b) What temptation does Deut. 8:17 warn against?
   c) Note the phrase "you may say to yourself". Discuss the notion that the sin discussed in this verse may not always manifest itself in bombastic external statements, but rather that it is a condition of the heart.
3) Do you agree or disagree with the summary on p. 8?
4) There are numerous references to 'not forget God" in the O.T.
   a) Using a concordance, look up some of them.
   b) Discuss the statement, "Forgetting God is best understood as a *moral* act rather than a *mental* one."
   c) Read Jer. 2:32. Would your own behaviour identify you as one of the people of God whom Jeremiah is addressing?
5) The hymn writer put it this way:
   "O to grace how great a debtor,
   Daily I'm constrained to be
   Let thy grace, Lord, like a fetter,
   Bind my wandering heart to thee,

Prone to wander, Lord, I feel it,
Prone to leave the God I love.
Here's my heart, Lord, O take and seal it,
Seal it for thy courts above."

a) Do you believe this is a normal Christian
   experience?
b) To what extent can you identify with this hymn?

Deut. 26:1 -11

1) What does this passage say concerning redemption (26:
   8-10) and the blessings that come from God's created
   world (26: 5 -10)?
2) What blessings are named in vss. 9 & 10?
3) How might a thanksgiving service be structured so that
   both the spiritual and material aspects of the gospel are
   integrated into the service?

Proverbs 3: 9-10

1) "The Church is always asking for money." How might
   such an accusation be answered by this biblical text?
2) Do you think that the use of our money is an important
   sign of our discipleship?
3) If so, how should it be used by a disciple of Christ?
4) As a follower of Jesus, how is *your* use of money
   different from that of the world?
5) Why do you suppose that Christians called to *sacrificial*
   giving? See I John 2: 15-17.
6) See also I Sam. 2: 30b. Are you passionate about using
   your wealth to bring honour and glory to God?

VIII. STUDY QUESTIONS

7) Using a concordance, read and study 'firstfruits'. In what way do you suppose that the giving of our firstfruits is an act of faith?

I Chronicles 29:10 -18

1) How can David's attitude of humility in giving personally to the building of the temple (vs. 14) be reproduced in our lives today?
2) Why should we feel humbled by the privilege of giving?
3) Have you experienced humility in giving? If not, how might you embrace such an attitude in your own life?
4) Compare II Cor. 8:4.
   a) What phrase in David's prayer (vs. 17) provides evidence of his humility?
   b) The adverb 'willingly' indicates emphasis in vs. 17.
5) Compare II Cor. 8:11; what is Paul urging here?
6) Compare and discuss this same thought as expounded in Exod. 25:2; I Chron. 28:9; Ezra 6:6 and Ps. 110:3a.

Psalm 49

1) Read Psalm 49 and summarize what it teaches about wealth.
2) According to vss.1-4 to whom is this psalm being addressed?

Malachi 3:8-12

1) Discuss the connection between the call to repentance and giving.

2) Since repentance is usually seen as an *emotional* response, such as in cases of adultery, social injustice, etc., what is the difference expected in Malachi?
   a) What does Malachi reveal that the Lord is doing with us through our giving?
   b) Does this passage provide us with an iron-clad formula for material success? Discuss.
   c) What are the real basic principles about faith and giving that are revealed in Malachi?
3) What is the great robbery in Malachi?
4) Who are the victims of the great robbery?

Proverbs

1) Proverbs is one of many O.T. books containing passages about the possible idolatry of wealth.
   a) Read Ps. 48:6; Deut. 32:20; Jer. 9:23-24 and Prov. 18:11.
   b) Pray together over these verses and acknowledge your need of God to overcome idolatry if present.
   c) What supportive role can fellow Christians play in this struggle?
2) Read Ps. 73:1-14. What does it reveal about attitudes towards the wealth or health of others?
3) Read Eccles. 5:10. What factors contribute to wealth being unsatisfying?
4) Proverbs contains a number of statements about the instability and uncertainty of wealth and about expending excessive energy to amass it.
   a) Compare Prov. 23:4-5 and I Tim.6:17 and discuss at what point you think a person has crossed the line between hard work and "wearing oneself out" to gain wealth.
   b) Can you identify with that struggle in your life?
   c) Do you discuss this among family members?

      d) A similar term is used to warn against "excessive eagerness" to obtain wealth in Prov. 11:1; 27:20; 28:20.

5) How might social injustice as noted in Amos 8:4-6 and Micah 2:1-2 be the result of this excessiveness?

6) Read Jer. 22:13-17. How relevant are these warnings for our contemporary business practices?

7) Read Mal. 3:5. How does a lack of fearing God lead to such societal breakdowns?

8) Consult Prov. 17:5; 22:16; 22:9, 22-23. How would a biblical view of men and women made in the image of God impact social, legal and economic injustice?

'Better Than' Sayings

1) It is sometimes said that Proverbs promises that godliness will lead to financial prosperity.
      a) What light do the 'better than' sayings shed on this idea?
      b) Why is wealth identified in Scripture as a substitute for God?
      c) Discuss how the four 'better than(s)' are expressed or implemented in your life.

2) The poet Yeats said, "Men and women are in love with what is vanishing. What more is there to say?"
      a) Is covetousness a problem for you?
      b) What do you do to overcome it?

The Bright Side of Wealth

1) How is God honored by our wealth?

2) Review Prov. 3: 9-10 and 14:31b and discuss them.

3) The Old and New Testaments demonstrate not only a God-centered life but equally an other-person-centered

view of life. Provide and discuss examples. (Think about the two divisions of the Ten Commandments).
4) Meditate upon and discuss I John 3;17 and I John 4:20,21.
   a) How would you express the relationship between loving God and your neighbor?
5) What should our relationship be to the gifts of creation with which we are blessed?
   a) What should such blessing lead to?
   b) Look at Eccles. 5:19. What is the difference between blessings as *pleasures* and *goals*?
6) Read I Cor. 3:9a. Giving allows us to participate with God in the work of his kingdom.
   a) Do you see yourself as participating with God in the ministry of giving?
   b) How would the idea of participation with God help us to understand both privilege and responsibility involved in our giving?
7) Part of the bright side of wealth is its use.
   a) Do you make a dichotomy between giving to God and giving to people? If so, is this correct, and if not, why not?
   b) Make an argument for the proposition that there is no difference between the provisions of the O.T. laws to care for and protect the poor, unfair weights (Amos 8:4-6), unjust courts (Isa. 10:1-3) and religious rulers (Micah 3:1-2) and N.T. precepts for such cases.
   c) Why do you think that a godly use of our wealth and godly concern for the oppressed and disadvantaged permeates the Pentateuch, Prophets, Psalms and Wisdom Literature? [There are too many verses to be included here but any good resource material on social justice could be consulted and become a basis for a serious interaction with this issue.]

8) Two texts on the source of wealth must be integrated into a biblical philosophy: Proverbs 10:4-5 and 13:4 praise diligence in work and at the same time instruct us that, "it is the blessing of the Lord that brings wealth and he adds no trouble with it" (10:22).
   a) How do you see this conjunction of divine and human factors in your life?
   b) Does such a duality operate in other biblical themes; if so, which?
   c) Discuss C. Wright's comment: "The whole of scripture rules out the notion that it is hard work *alone*, apart from our God-given abilities that should receive the credit."

III. The Prosperity Gospel

1) "God has made provision for all believers to be wealthy. Believers wealth is determined by their faith."
   a) Perhaps you have seen preachers on television taking this position. Do you have friends or fellow church members who believe this?
   b) Why might it be popular?
   c) What does the prosperity gospel teach us about the importance of considering the whole of scripture, about comparing scripture with scripture and about "searching (examining) the scriptures everyday to see (Acts. 17:11) what the truth is?
2) Using a concordance look up the words *prosperous* and *success*.
   a) What is their context?
   b) Are they referring to material or spiritual success?
   c) Read III John 2 and discuss what 'go well with you' means.

3) Discuss the following: "Proverbs consistently insists that righteousness outweighs wealth and that wickedness renders wealth worthless.
4) Discuss whether or not wealth has any intrinsic or universal good.
5) The book of Proverbs describes both the benefits and the dangers of wealth.
   a) Using a concordance find the texts in Proverbs that warn of the dangers of wealth and those that deal with its blessings.
   b) In what contexts may wealth be understood as a good thing?
   c) In what contexts may wealth be understood as a bad thing?
   d) Discuss whether or not it is wise to isolate the blessings from warnings of the dangers, in the manner of the prosperity gospel?
6) Literarily, Proverbs follows a style which majors in tersely expressed sayings. These sayings are then qualified by subsequent Proverbs. See Proverbs 26:4-5. Since many of the qualifications are scattered throughout the book, they are easily overlooked. Using a concordance find some of the contrasting qualifications of wealth as blessing and temptation.
7) If wealth is a unique blessing promised by God, how would one explain Prov. 11:4?
8) If riches can be claimed by faith why are there so many warnings about their dangers in the O.T?
9) Two themes in Proverbs put the lie to the prosperity gospel. One is the 'better than' statements already discussed. The second is the extensive use of the central promise of 'life' in the book, ie. *fellowship with God.* Use a concordance to find texts demonstrating or disproving this.

VIII. STUDY QUESTIONS

IV. Jesus and Wealth

1) In Luke 16:11 Jesus contrasts worldly wealth with true riches. What do you think Jesus meant by 'worldly wealth'?
2) Discuss the following: The world asks, "What does a man own?"; Christ asks, "How does he use it?"; The world thinks more about money-getting; Christ, about the money-giving. And when a man gives, the world still asks, "*What* does he give?"; Christ asks, "*How* does he give?"; The world looks at the money and its amount; Christ looks at the man and his motive."
3) Reflect on Phil. 3: 19, especially the end clause "whose mind is set on present earthly things". This is how the opponents of the cross live. They have abandoned a lifestyle marked by the cross.
4) Consider Luke 16:14-15. The Pharisees loved money and sneered at Jesus. Why do you suppose they sneered at Jesus?
5) Name other things that are highly valued among men.
6) Do you believe we take seriously Jesus' radical statements on money, such as Matt. 16:26 or 19:22-23?
   a) Study the parable in Luke 12:13-21.
   b) What was wrong with the wealthy agri-businessman building bigger barns?
   c) Was Jesus only talking about wealthy farmers?
   d) What is the application to us?
   e) Discuss Jesus' concluding statement in vs. 21, paying special attention to the word *anyone*.
7) Luke 16:19-31, the story of the rich man and Lazarus, the beggar, is one of the best-known of Jesus' stories.
   a) Pick out from it some of the clear lessons.
   b) What in the story tells you anything about the character of the rich man?
   c) What is the significance of 16:30 and 31, particularly the latter?

Matt.19; Mark 10; Luke 18

8) What might we surmise about the rich young ruler's attitude in coming to Jesus with his question?

9) What was good or not so good about his question?

10) How would you account for the difference in the way Jesus responded to this question compared to that asked in John 6:28-29?

11) What might be surmised about Jesus changing the order of commandments six to ten?

12) Is there any certainty about the young ruler's attitude or behavior towards his parents?

13) How do you feel about and what is your response to Jesus' severe statement in Mark 10:23?

14) In what areas of our lives other than money might it be necessary to sacrifice for the sake of attaining eternal life?

15) What do you think about the 100 to 1 person comparison, in adversity and prosperity?

16) Do you think Jesus' statement, in response to the disciples' question, "Who, then ..?" applies across the board to all persons or just to the class of rich that Jesus is talking about?

Mark 12:41-44

1) Reflect on Jesus watching the crowd as they gave, vs. 41.

    a) Do you find that challenging or threatening?

    b) Do you think that we might give more generously and sacrificially if we were conscious of being watched by Jesus in our giving?

    c) What is the major lesson about giving we should come away with from this passage?

VIII. STUDY QUESTIONS

V. Paul and Wealth

I Cor. 16:1-4.

1) Paul was exercised about a collection of money to be sent to the poor churches in Jerusalem. One writer using this passage calls the teaching here 'a carefully designed program of stewardship'.
2) Do you agree? Why or why not?
3) What clear principles to be followed on giving are found here?

II Corinthians 8 & 9

1) This is the Apostle Paul's most extensive treatment on the subject of giving. Put in your own words the principal teachings found here.
2) Which statement in these chapters would you rank as highest in importance?
3) Was anything said about the O.T. tithes?
   a) What does this say to us?
   b) How critical is an argument from silence?

I Tim. 6:6-10

1) Discuss your perception of our western secular culture's attitudes towards wealth and charity.
2) Discuss the methods our culture uses to promote its attitudes towards wealth and materialism.
3) Are we conscious enough of being influenced by our culture?
4) How does our culture affect your giving?

5) Do we take seriously Jesus' statement in Matt. 6: 19-21 which suggests earthly treasure may block our vision of the heavenly treasure?
6) What do you think heavenly treasure consists of?
7) What is Paul's focus in I Tim. 7-8?
8) What are the dangers of wealth mentioned in this passage?
9) Make a list and pray over them.
10) What is it about our culture which militates against taking these warnings seriously?
11) Such warnings were given already in the O.T.; compare the dangers mentioned there with those found in this passage.
12) How might the apostle have been influenced by his knowledge of the O.T?

I Timothy 6:17-19

1) Paul speaks of riches being uncertain (vs. 17).
   a) What might he be thinking that makes wealth uncertain?
   b) Wealth gives people a false feeling of security. See Prov. 10:15 and 18:11 and compare these with Prov. 18:10.
   c) Where is the believer's true security to be found?
2) Paul exhorts the rich to use their wealth to do good (6:18). The wealthy may theoretically have more opportunity to do good to others but *all* who are believers are also exhorted "to be eager to do what is good" (Titus 2:14b).
   a) What is Paul's motivation in exhorting the rich in this passage?
   b) What relation does his belief in 'heavenly treasure' have to Jesus' statement in Matt. 6:19?

VI. Comparisons between the Testaments

1) Are believers living in the N.T. period more, less, or similarly accountable for their lifestyle than O.T. believers? See Matt. 11:11; 13:16-17 and I Peter 1:12.
2) Does the question of financial *accountability* affect the question of whether or not the O.T. tithe carries over into the New Covenant?
3) The question of the carryover of the O.T. tithe into the New Covenant period must be answered in the light of the following issues:
   a) What do you think the Bible teaches about the law of tithing as a direct carry over from the O.T. into the New Covenant as a means to provide support for temple centered worship?
   b) Do you think any principles associated with tithing are transferable from the O.T. to the New Covenant?
   c) Do you think that those who support the O.T. law of tithing as a principle for 'giving' today, are indeed applying the O.T. tithe both in the form and for the purpose for which God intended it, or have both form and intent been altered?
      i) How much was the O.T. tithe; 10 % or 23%?
      ii) Were the 'tithes and offerings' part of the ceremonial law as in Mal. 3 or not?
      iii) Was the existence of the tithe perhaps being presupposed by Paul or seen by Paul as being superseded by the principles of giving? This should be discussed in the context of the following two facts: Paul was dealing with Gentile churches with no connection to Jerusalem Temple centered worship. The significance of the appearance of the Christ and it's implications on the continuation or

termination of temple centered worship and the priesthood.

4) Some see the tithe as one of the secrets of church growth. What do you think about this?

5) On the opposite side is the opinion that tithing in N. America is a middle-class way of robbing God, if accompanied by the position that the rest belongs to 'me and my family'. What is your opinion about this?

6) Ron Sider's proposed graduated tithe means the more we earn the more we give. What is your opinion about this?

VII. How Then Shall We Give?

1) What do you think of the statement that "God increases our standard of living so that we may increase our standard of giving"?

2) Perhaps the most critically important question to us today is the question, "Who are today's rich?" How might we try to determine that biblically? Do you believe that when a person is converted their pocketbook should also be converted, or rather that "when money speaks, truth is silent"?

3) Comment on and discuss the following:
   a) "How we use our money demonstrates the reality of our love for God. In some ways it proves our love more conclusively than depth of knowledge, length of prayers or prominence of service."
   b) "There are two ways in which a Christian may view his money - How much of my money shall I use for God? Or , How much of God's money shall I use for myself?

IX. Recommended Readings

Alcorn, Randy, *The Law of Rewards*

Ellul, Jacques, *Money and Power*

Fee, Gordon, *The Disease of the Health and Wealth Gospel*

Foster, Richard, *Money, Sex and Power*

Getz, Gene, *A Biblical Theology of Material Possessions*

Kaiser, Walter, *Toward Old Testament Ethics,* chap.13

Murray, Andrew, *Christ's Perspective on the Use and Abuse of Money*

Sider, Ron, *Rich Christians in an Age of Hunger*

White, John, *The Sacred Cow*

Printed in the United States
85028LV00005B/298-369/A

9 781894 667869